David
and Goliath

Story by Penny Frank

Illustrated by Tony Morris

THE LION
STORY BIBLE

18

OXFORD · BATAVIA · SYDNEY

The Bible tells us how God chose the Israelites to be his special people. He made them a promise that he would always love and care for them. But they must obey him.

In this story God uses David to show his people what trusting God really means. You can find the story in your own Bible, in the first book of Samuel, chapter 17.

Copyright © 1986 Lion Publishing

Published by
Lion Publishing plc
Sandy Lane West, Littlemore, Oxford, England
ISBN 0 85648 743 0
ISBN 0 7459 1763 1 (paperback)
Lion Publishing Corporation
1705 Hubbard Avenue, Batavia, Illinois 60510, USA
ISBN 0 85648 743 0
Albatross Books Pty Ltd
PO Box 320, Sutherland, NSW 2232, Australia
ISBN 0 86760 527 8
ISBN 0 7324 0083 X (paperback)

First edition 1986, reprinted 1987, 1988
Paperback edition 1989

British Library Cataloguing in Publication Data

Frank, Penny
David and Goliath. – (The Lion Story
Bible; v. 18)
1. David, *King of Israel* – Juvenile
literature 2. Goliath – Juvenile
literature 3. Bible stories.
English – O.T. Samuel, 1st
I. Title   II. Morris, Tony
1938 Aug 2 –
222′.430922   BS580.D3

ISBN 0-85648-743-0
ISBN 0-7459-1763-1 (paperback)

Printed in Yugoslavia

Library of Congress Cataloging in Publication Data

Frank, Penny.
David and Goliath.
(The Lion Story Bible; 18)
1. David, King of Israel – Juvenile
literature. 2. Goliath (Biblical giant) –
Juvenile literature. [1. David, King of
Israel 2. Goliath (Biblical giant)
3. Bible stories – O.T.] I. Morris, Tony,
ill. II. Title. III. Series: Frank, Penny.
Lion Story Bible; 18.
BS580.D3F68 1986   222′.4309505
85-24109
ISBN 0-85648-743-0
ISBN 0-7459-1763-1 (paperback)

David was the youngest of eight sons.
His father was a shepherd called Jesse.
    When David was growing up, the
prophet Samuel visited Jesse's family. He
told them that, when King Saul died,
David would be the next king of Israel.

God had especially chosen him, so
David knew that God was with him in a
special way.

David worked hard.

'God has to teach me to be a really
good shepherd before he can make me a
good king,' he said.

David played the harp and sang his own
songs about God. King Saul sometimes
asked David to go to the palace and sing
for him. When the king was in a bad
mood, David's songs made him feel
better.

David's brothers were soldiers. They fought in King Saul's army. They were often away from home for a long time.

Their father was pleased that David was at home to keep him company. He was an old man and David helped him look after the sheep.

David often spent days and nights out
on the hills. He had to take the sheep to
places where there was grass and water.

There were lions, wild bears and
wolves living in the hills. David was
sometimes afraid.

He had to fight off the wild animals
to keep the lambs and sheep safe.

One day when David came back from
the hills, his father said, 'You can leave
the sheep for one of the men to look
after. I want you to go to visit your
brothers. Take them some good food and
bring me back news of them.'

So David packed some food and set off on the journey.

It was a long way, but David knew the hills very well.

At last he found his brothers with the Israelite army. They looked really frightened.

'What's the matter?' David asked.

They pointed to the hill across the valley. 'Over there, with the Philistine soldiers, is the giant Goliath,' they said. 'He wants one of us to fight him.'

'Well, why don't you?' asked David.
'You are the army of the living God. You will win.'

'If you're so brave, then come and tell the king you'll go,' sneered the brothers.

They were very surprised when David did just as they said. He told the king that he would go to fight Goliath, and that God would fight for him.

'You must have my helmet and sword,' said King Saul.

But everything was so heavy that David could not stand up.

'I can't wear this,' David said, 'I'll just take the sling and stones I use when I am a shepherd.'

He took his sling and carefully chose five smooth stones from beside the stream.

When Goliath saw David walking across
the valley towards him, he laughed so
loudly that the Israelites had to cover up
their ears.

Goliath had a sword and a shield.

But when he saw that David had
brought only stones and a sling, he was
angry.

'Do you think you are only fighting to
keep your sheep safe?' he jeered.

But David knew how to fight with
stones. He took out his sling as he
walked. He fitted a stone into it.

When he was close to Goliath he
shouted, 'I come against you in the
name of the living God!'

David swung the sling around and around above his head. When he let go, the stone flew out and hit Goliath on his forehead. It was just the one place where he could be hurt.

The stone killed Goliath.

David drew the giant's own sword and
cut off his head.

When the Philistines saw that Goliath
was dead, they ran away.

The Israelites cheered when they saw what David had done to Goliath. They ran after the Philistines, driving them out of their land.

All the Israelites heard that David had won the battle. They knew the Philistines had run away.

They danced in the streets and sang songs about David, the brave shepherd.

King Saul grew jealous because everyone was talking about David.

David had learned to trust God when he was a shepherd. Now he had killed a giant because he knew that the God of Israel was the living God, who helps his people.

David would know how to trust God when he became king.

The Lion Story Bible is made up of 52 individual stories for young readers, building up an understanding of the Bible as one story — God's story — a story for all time and all people.

The Old Testament section (numbers 1–30) tells the story of a great nation — God's chosen people, the Israelites — and God's love and care for them through good times and bad. The stories are about people who knew and trusted God. From this nation came one special person, Jesus Christ, sent by God to save all people everywhere.

The story of *David and Goliath* comes from one of the Old Testament history books: 1 Samuel, chapter 17. It is not simply a story of a boy against a giant. The important thing was not David's size but his trust in God. He was not afraid to face Goliath, unarmed except for his shepherd's sling, because he knew that God could protect him.

'I come against you in the name of the Lord Almighty,' he said. 'Today . . . all those gathered here will know that it is not by sword or spear that the Lord saves; for the battle is the Lord's, and he will give all of you into our hands.'

The next story in the series, number 19: *King David*, tells how the shepherd boy became a great king.